Take Part

Take
One

Joan Burgen

Stanley Thornes (Publishers) Ltd

First published in 1986 by:
Stanley Thornes (Publishers) Ltd
Old Station Drive
Leckhampton
CHELTENHAM GL53 0DN
England

British Library Cataloguing in Publication Data

Burgen, J.
    Take part: take one.
    Pupils' bk.
    1. Drama in education   2. Education,
    Secondary
    I. Title
    792′.07′12   PN3171

    ISBN 0-85950-557-X

Typeset by Tech Set, Gateshead, Tyne & Wear,
in $10\frac{1}{2}/12\frac{1}{2}$ Palatino, and $10\frac{1}{2}/12\frac{1}{2}$ Optima.
Printed and bound in Great Britain by Ebenezer Baylis & Son Ltd, Worcester.

CONTENTS

ACKNOWLEDGEMENTS

We are grateful to Grace Jackson Penny for permission to reproduce 'How the Seven Brothers Saved their Sister' from *Tales of the Cheyenne*, and to BBC Hulton Picture Library, Barnaby's Picture Library and the Keystone Press Agency Ltd. for providing us with prints and granting permission to reproduce them.

I KNOW WHAT I LIKE

Airport

SITUATION

Each of the characters described below is waiting in the airport passenger lounge. They are due to board different flights – all of which have been delayed. From the huge windows in the passenger lounge you can see planes being towed to the outskirts of the airfield, and fire-engines and covered trucks, lining up alongside the main runway.

Choose one of the characters below for yourself. Read carefully the details about your character and decide on a name for yourself. Discuss with the rest of your group who you are, and what you are like.

When the drama starts, you will have to react to everything that happens as if you really were the person you have chosen to be.

CHARACTERS

Football Fans. (Not more than four.) You are going to see your favourite team play Real Madrid. You have been saving up for this trip for months and you want to enjoy yourself. You have seen all the publicity about football hooligans in the papers and on the television – you think it is very one sided. No one has explained what it really feels like to support a team. You don't consider yourselves to be violent people.

Businessman. You are not very pleased. Your secretary forgot to book you a first class seat and now the flight has been delayed. You will be late for your meeting in Rome. You have been under a lot of pressure lately and you have been working too hard. It's been weeks since you've had time to relax.

Businessman's Secretary. You aren't very pleased either. Your boss is grumpy because you didn't book a first class seat for him. You know he's been under a lot of pressure but then so have you. At least when he gets home he has a wife to look after him – you have two small children to look after. You *need* this job.

The Naseem Family. The family includes father, mother, two daughters and a younger son. The immigration authorities have decided that the family are illegal immigrants because when you originally came to this country, more than eleven years ago, you did not sign the correct documents. There has been widespread publicity about your case, and you are hoping that there might be a last-minute reprieve. You had a thriving business in East London which employed thirty workers.

Girl in the Lounge Coffee Bar. You are fed up with this job. You've seen so many people in the last few months that they are just a blur to you now. You know that there have been complaints about the way you serve the customers but you don't care.

Elderly Lady. You are going to visit your married daughter who now lives in Singapore. You have never travelled by air before and you are very nervous. People have always fascinated you – you spend a lot of time watching them. You have guessed, for instance, that the young man sitting next to you is involved in some sort of crime.

Young Man. You are carrying a half kilo packet of heroin in your hand baggage. You know that you are committing a crime but your sister has become addicted to the drug and the people who supply her have said that they will cut off her supply if you don't make this trip for them. You are desperate to help her but you don't know what to do.

Young French Woman. You are going home after a year's work in Britain as an au pair girl. You haven't been very happy in this country and you can't wait to get home to France.

Two Brothers. You are going to visit your parents for the school holidays. Your father works for an international company and is sent all over the world, so the two of you go to a boarding school in England. You

are very close to each other. Your favourite pastime is playing practical jokes.

Security Staff. Male and female. The whole airport is on alert because a man has hijacked a plane and directed it to this airport. Your job is to make sure that the man is taken into custody once the plane lands and to prevent any panic among the passengers. You have also been warned by the local police that someone in the passenger lounge is a drug smuggler.

Cleaners. You know something is going on and you want to find out what it is. You are going to try to listen in to conversations – this will be quite easy to do because people tend not to take much notice of you as you go about your job.

Two Young Women. You are both 18 and work in a travel agency. One of you is only interested in finding a man and getting married. The other is increasingly fed up with this and is beginning to regret ever deciding to go on holiday.

Second Young Man. You have been unemployed for nearly two years. You are going to France because you have heard there are jobs there. You don't speak French and you have no idea what the conditions of work are like there.

Quickies

That's me

Each person writes a description of themselves on a piece of card in such a way that it could be no other person in the group. Try to describe ideas and personality as well as just physical appearance.

Each person then reads out their own card to the group who have to decide whether or not the description really fits him or her. Revise the description until you are all satisfied that it expresses everything that is unique about the person. No one else should be able to say, 'That sounds like me!'

Making faces

Sit together in a circle. The leader of the group chooses one of the following emotions and points to any person in the circle who then has to 'make' a face to express the emotion.

Sorrow	Astonishment	Indifference
Worry	Shame	Triumph
Carefreeness	Amusement	Weariness
Terror	Impatience	Hatred

Throwing faces

Sit together in a circle. One person 'puts on' a smiling face. Then the face is carefully 'peeled off' and thrown to another person in the circle. This person then 'puts on' the face, before again 'peeling' it off to throw to someone else.

Variation. Throw other kinds of faces – worried, fearful, angry etc.

Amoeba

Have three sets of pairs in the group while the rest remain separate from each other. The pairs are the 'amoebae' and the rest of the class is their food. The 'amoebae' will chase and try to catch you – but they can only 'eat' you by passing their linked hands over your head, thereby holding you in the circle made by their hands. Once you have been eaten you become part of the amoeba. The largest amoeba is the winner.

Starting Points

Fit for the job?

Work in groups of five. One person is going to be interviewed for a job by the other four members of the group. The job is to take 30 children to summer camp for three weeks.

Before the interview choose a favourite character from television, books, films or plays. You will answer all the interviewers' questions as if you were that person. Their task is to find out who you are. The only question they cannot ask of course is, 'Who are you?'

Dressed to kill (role play)

CHARACTERS

Teenager
Parent
Sales assistant

SITUATION

The teenager and parent are in town looking for an outfit for the teenager to wear for his/her first job interview. They are in the teenage section of a large department store where the sales assistant is trying to help them.

Number one

You are going to produce a complete promotional campaign for a song or record. The first thing to do is to choose a record. It helps if it isn't very well known – you could even write your own!

Divide the tasks below between separate small groups. When each group has finished their task put everything together as your promotion.

a) Video. Improvise a short scene with action, movement and dance, to fit the lyrics of the song.
b) Write a review of the record. Write it in the same style as those you read in magazines.
c) Design posters and album sleeve.
d) Write a script for a DJ to read, before the record is played on the radio.

Variation. Do the whole thing as a parody. Take a well known and fairly serious song ('Land of Hope and Glory' or the National Anthem might work) and promote it like a pop song.

MEMORIES

How the Seven Brothers Saved their Sister

Long and long ago, there lived among the Cheyennes an old woman and her young granddaughter. They had no other relatives, and lived together in a little lodge, where the grandmother taught the young girl, Red Leaf, to make fine beaded robes and moccasins. Nowhere in all the tribe was there a better robe-maker than Red Leaf.

Now it so happened that not very far from there lived seven brothers. They had no father, no mother, and no sisters. The seven of them lived together, with the youngest, Moksois, staying at home to take care of the camp while the six older brothers went out to hunt.

'Grandmother,' said Red Leaf, one day, 'I would like to have Moksois and his brothers to be my brothers. They are great hunters, and could bring home food for us all. They have no sister, so I could keep their lodge, and cook their food, and make their moccasins.'

Her grandmother thought that was a fine idea, so she helped Red Leaf select seven of her nicest robes, and seven pairs of her best moccasins. These she carried over to the lodge of the seven brothers.

The six brothers were hunting, and Moksois was down at the creek getting water when she came to the lodge, but she went in,

anyway, and put one of the robes and a pair of moccasins on each of the seven beds. When he got back with the water, she was stirring the pot of soup on the fire. They talked and then he saw the robes and the moccasins.

'Where did these fine moccasins and robes come from?' he asked.

'I brought them. I thought it would be a good thing for us all if I became your sister,' Red Leaf answered, still stirring the soup.

'It suits me,' Moksois said. 'But I'll have to ask my brothers about it.'

When the brothers came home from the hunt and found the fine new robes and moccasins, and learned that Red Leaf wanted to be their sister, they thought it was a good arrangement.

So that was the way it was, from then on. They all lived together, very comfortably. The brothers hunted, and Red Leaf took care of the meat they brought home, and made their robes and moccasins, and Moksois helped by bringing in water, and keeping plenty of wood for fire.

But there came a day when everything changed. Moksois took his bow and arrows and went out to hunt chipmunks. He wandered farther from the lodge than he thought. While he was gone, a giant buffalo bull came to the lodge and took Red Leaf and ran away with her.

He was the Double-Teethed Bull, strange mysterious bull, strongest of all the buffalo. He was different from the other buffalo, for he had teeth in his upper and in his lower jaw, and he ruled over them.

When Moksois returned to the lodge, he found it partly torn down, and the tracks of the great bull coming in and going out. He was very much afraid. Tears ran down his face while he searched for his sister. When he saw his brothers coming home from the hunt, he ran to them, crying, 'A great bull has stolen our sister.'

The brothers knew the tracks were those of a great Double-Teethed Bull. They began to mourn and cry, 'What can we do to save our sister? The Double-Teethed Bull is so powerful we can do nothing against him. He cannot be killed.'

At last, one said, 'We can't just sit here. Let's get busy and build four strong corrals[1] one inside the other. Then we'll go and try to get our sister away from him. That way, if we can get her, we will have some strong place to bring her.'

This they did, piling big logs together and bracing them like a fort. When all four were finished, little Moksois went out and gathered anthills and brought them back in his robe. He scattered the ants and sand in a line all around the inside of the smallest corral.

Then the seven brothers followed the tracks of their sister and the great bull for a long time. At last they came to the top of a high hill, from which they could look far across the plain. There they saw a great herd of buffalo, covering the plain as far as the eye could see. In the centre of the herd was a large open space, and in the open space sat their sister, with the great bull lying on the ground close by. No other buffalo were near them.

The brothers had brought their medicine sacks with them. One was made from the skin of a blackbird, one from that of a crow, one from a coyote skin, and one from the skin of a tiny yellow bird. Little Moksois' medicine sack was made of tanned buffalo hide, made in the shape of a half-moon, and he carried the skin of a gopher[2] inside it.

The eldest brother took the blackbird skin in his hand, and it changed into a live blackbird. He told the bird to fly down and try to get close enough to their sister to tell her they were there.

He flew close to Red Leaf, where she sat on the ground, half-covered by her robe. He tried to talk to her, but the great bull saw him there and rumbled, 'Blackbird, what are you trying to do? Are you a spy? Go away, or I will look at you and you will fall to the ground, dead.' The blackbird was afraid of his power, so he flew back to the brothers.

The second brother sent the coyote that came alive from the coyote-skin medicine sack. The coyote was very clever. He slipped around far to the south, and came up on the other side of the herd. Then he went limping through the buffalo, acting as though he were sick and crippled.

But the Double-Teethed Bull was not fooled. He shook his heavy horns at him and said, 'Coyote, I think you are a spy. Go away, before I look at you and you die . . .'

[1] cattle enclosure made of log fencing.

[2] small, burrowing animal, rather like a squirrel.

So coyote was afraid to stay. He went back to the brothers. This time they tried the crow. He flew in close, lighting on the ground, and pecking as though gathering food, then flying a little closer and lighting again. But the bull suspected him. 'Go away crow. Don't come any closer. You're trying to do something bad. I think I'll just look at you. Then you'll fall down dead . . .' Crow didn't wait. He flew away, back to the brothers, waiting on the hill.

The last to go was the tiny yellow bird. He was so tiny that he crept along through the grass, among the buffalo, without any of them seeing him, even the great bull. He slipped under Red Leaf's robe and said to her, 'Red Leaf, your brothers are yonder on the hill. They will try to save you. They sent me to tell you what to do. Just cover yourself all over with your robe, and pretend to go to sleep. Then wait.'

The great bull snorted, and rumbled in his throat, but he didn't see the little yellow bird as he crept back through the herd. When he got back to the hill the brothers took council among themselves. Moksois said, 'Now it is my turn to do something. Everyone be quiet. I will try to put the Double-Teethed Bull to sleep so we can do something.'

So he lay down on the ground with his half-moon medicine sack by his head and shut his eyes. Everyone kept very still, waiting. After a time he opened his eyes and arose. 'Blackbird, fly down and see if the bull is asleep,' he said.

When the blackbird came back, he said he'd seen the great bull sleeping soundly, with his nose against the ground.

'That is good,' said Moksois. 'I am to blame for the Double-Teethed Bull stealing our sister. Now I will get her back. All of you wait here, but be ready to run away when I get back.'

He opened his half-moon medicine sack and took the gopher skin out and laid it on the ground. Instantly, it became a live gopher, and started to dig with its long sharp claws. Moksois stayed right beside the gopher and followed it into the hole it was digging.

The gopher made a tunnel straight to where Red Leaf lay, covered by her robe. Moksois came up under the robe and took her by the hand and led her back along the gopher hole to where the brothers waited.

They took their sister, and as fast as they could, they ran toward home, to the shelter of the strong corrals they had built. But Moksois stayed behind, to keep watch on the herd. He wanted to see what happened when the great bull found Red Leaf gone. He felt very brave. 'I will stay here and watch,' he said. 'I am not afraid. Let the Double-Teethed Bull look at me. He can't kill me with one of his looks.'

The great bull heaved himself to his feet and shook himself all over. Then he walked over to Red Leaf's robe, still spread out on the ground over the gopher hole, and sniffed at it. When he saw she was gone, he bellowed and pawed the ground, throwing clouds of dust into the air. He tossed and hooked the robe with his sharp horns until he tore it to shreds.

All the buffalo were excited and milling around, pawing and bellowing. Then the bull saw the gopher hole. He sniffed at it then began to run back over the ground in the same direction Moksois and Red Leaf had gone through the tunnel. All the other buffalo followed him, charging at great speed; heads down, stirring up such a cloud of dust that it was like the smoke from a prairie fire.

Moksois watched them from the hill, but before they got too near, he put an arrow in his bow and shot it as far as he could, toward home. The instant the arrow touched the ground, Moksois was beside it. That was part of his power. He kept shooting his arrows until he reached the lodge.

'Get ready, the buffalo are coming,' he cried. And they all got inside the log corrals and kept watch. In a little while, the great herd of buffalo came in sight, galloping over the plain, with the huge bull out in front. When they saw the corrals, they stopped and waited while an old cow walked slowly nearer.

'Come back with me, Red Leaf. The Double-Teethed Bull wants you,' she called to them. 'If you don't return, he will come and get you himself.'

Moksois said, 'Tell him to come, if he dares.' But before she had gone very far, he shot the old cow, and she fell to the ground. Three other messengers came, asking Red Leaf to come back to the Double-Teethed Bull, and making threats. Each time Moksois gave them the same answer. Each time he shot them before they got back to the great bull. Only the last one got near enough to give him Moksois' message.

Then the great bull was terribly angry. He pranced and pawed. He hooked the ground and bellowed defiance. Head down, he charged the corral at a fast gallop, the herd thundering behind.

'Come out,' he roared to the girl. 'Come out. Don't you know who I am?'

Red Leaf was trembling and crying. She begged her brothers to let her go. 'He will kill you all. Let me go . . . It may save you . . .'

But Moksois said, 'Don't be afraid. Don't cry. I will kill the bull.'

When the Double-Teethed Bull heard Moksois say that, he was furious. He charged the corral and hooked his horns in the logs,

tossing them aside like sticks. The churning, bellowing herd charged the other corrals, one after another, scattering the logs like straw in the wind. But when they came to the place where Moksois had made the line inside with the anthills, every grain of sand had become a big rock, making a strong rock corral that stopped the buffalo charge.

Again and again the buffalo charged the wall, hurling the great stones in every direction, like pebbles. The eldest brother said, 'Even these rocks can't stand against him. He will be inside, next time . . .'

Their sister cried, 'Let me go . . . let me go outside, or he will kill you all.'

But Moksois said again, 'Don't be afraid. Stay here. I still have power . . .' Then he shot his arrow straight up into the air, just as high as he could shoot it. And as high as it went, there stood a tall tree, reaching into the sky.

'Now, hurry, climb up there,' he cried, helping his sister into the tree. Quickly, all the brothers climbed up into the branches. But just as Moksois climbed to the lowest limb, the Double-Teethed Bull broke through the rocks with a terrible bellow that shook the hills.

He charged and charged the tree, tearing off great slivers with his sharp horns. But just as fast as he tossed a piece of wood aside it joined back to the tree the same as it had been before.

Moksois only waited to shoot his last arrow at the powerful bull, before he followed his brothers and his sister up and up the tree, until they went into the sky. There they became the seven stars. The girl is the head star, and the little one, off to one side by itself, is little Moksois, still keeping guard.

Cheyenne Indian myth

FOLLOW-UP

The Crow Indians, like many other Indian tribes, relied mainly on the spoken word for communication. Their history would have been passed down through the generations of the tribe by the story-tellers. The stories and poems which have survived (like the story you have just read), often seem too fantastic to be true; but far back in their history, they were probably based on a real event. Often the story-telling would form part of the religious rituals of the tribe.

1 This piece of drama is for the whole class.

a) Discuss:
● what kind of characters would you find in an Indian village?
● what work would they be doing?
● decide how your village is laid out and what sort of land surrounds it
● what time of year is it?
● have you enough food?
● if not, why not?
● has the game moved away or are your hunters sick (or inefficient)?
● is this a good time for the tribe?
● if not, why not?

b) Break up into groups and work out the characters in the group. Give yourself a name. Decide amongst yourselves what you were doing yesterday and what jobs need doing today. Start your work.

c) Night falls and gradually all the groups settle down to sleep.

d) A sound breaks through the dark – a familiar but still rather unnerving sound. This is part of the religious ritual of the tribe, and the Storyteller is only ever seen on these nights. No one knows who it is.

e) Everyone moves quickly and quietly to the circle in the centre of the village.

f) When the circle is made, the Storyteller suddenly appears, sits in the centre, and begins the tale of 'How the Seven Brothers saved their Sister'. (The person taking the part of the Storyteller can read the story or tell it from memory.)

2 Improvise the story of 'How the Seven Brothers saved their Sister'. You could use masks, mime and dancing in your improvisation – imagine the dance of the charging buffalo or a dance to show the building of the corral. Below are some simple ways that you can make masks.

a) A paper bag mask. This is just as it sounds. Get a *paper* bag large enough to go over your head. Make two holes for eyes and maybe one for your mouth. Use paints or felt tip pens to draw your character's face on the mask.

b) Stick masks. These are hand held. A piece of hardboard or stiff card large enough to cover your face is nailed to a small stick. Paint and cut the mask to be whatever you want.

c) Nose mask. Bend a semicircle of cardboard or stiff paper into a cone and secure the two straight edges with staples or sticky tape. Attach a piece of elastic to go round the back of your head. Nose masks can be made in any shape, size or colour – the odder the better!

d) Paper masks. These are rather more difficult. Use stiff cartridge paper for the best results but practice with newspaper until you are sure that you have a design you are satisfied with. Some paper masks are more complicated versions of nose masks (good for bird beaks).
One final point about masks – you must feel comfortable in them, otherwise you won't be able to move freely in them.

Quickies

Adding-up

Everyone sits in a circle. One person says,
 'I went shopping yesterday and bought
 a . . .'
The next person says,
 'I went shopping yesterday and bought a
 . . . and a . . .'
You can make up whatever you like to buy
but you have to remember to include every-
thing that has been bought up to your turn.
If you forget something, you must drop out.
As the list gets longer it becomes more and
more difficult to remember everything.

Notice anything?

Work with a partner – A and B. B must
look very carefully at A and try to remember every detail about A's appearance –
even things like the way hair falls, or whether
A is wearing a ring. Now while B's eyes are
shut A must change some small aspect of
his/her appearance. B will try to notice what
change has been made. Change places when
the difference has been detected.

Who's missing?

Everyone is scattered around the room at
random. One person, A, leaves the room.
Meanwhile B either hides or leaves the
room by another door. When A returns he
has to guess who is missing.

Helping with enquiries

Does your memory desert you if you suddenly have to remember exactly what you
were doing at a particular time? Try this in
threes or fours.

One person, A, is answering the questions
which are fired quickly at him by B, C and
D. They are trying to find out everything
that A has done in the last twenty-four
hours. Don't just ask when he had break-
fast, but also what he had to eat. If he says
he was in a particular lesson ask who sat in
front of him, what work was covered in the
class or what the teacher wore. Make sure
that your questions are as detailed as possible.

My story

Work in groups of five or six. (Call yourselves A, B, C etc.) A tells B about an incident which really happened to him. Then
B relates the incident to C as if it had happened to B, not A. C relates the tale to D –
and so on.

Discuss what happened to the story. Did it
change at all? How did A feel when other
people put themselves in *his* story?

Mime

Mime is not easy to do. Your movements
have to be clear and precise if you want
other people to get your message. One
way of beginning is to do everything in
slow motion – this helps you to understand
how many different stages there are, in
what seem to be very simple movements.
Try these to start with:
● drinking a cup of tea
● breaking an egg into a bowl
● tying a tie or shoelace.

A bit more difficult:
● applying make-up
● finding a slug in your trainers
● getting back to your seat in the cinema
 carrying a dripping ice cream.

Starting Points

Memories

Look at the pictures on the right and below. They could be scenes from the lives of the old couple in the last picture. Break up into groups. See if you can improvise scenes based on the pictures – you can add more characters if you think they would fit. Don't forget to ask yourselves questions about the characters you have chosen. You are more likely to get a better feeling of past times if you use mime, so you don't have to try to speak like people in the past.

FOLLOW-UP

You could join up the memories by using the old couple's conversation as a method of linking the different scenes and turning the whole thing into a performance.

What did you see?

Work in small groups to improvise a scene in which some sort of accident happens. It could involve a small child in the home, an incident in a school laboratory or an accident in the gym. (Try to avoid using car accidents since it's not too easy to improvise a car driving recklessly at 60 miles an hour!) Make sure that everyone in your group is quite sure about how the accident happened. Now perform your 'accident' for the rest of the class.

When all the 'accidents' have been seen, each group should question another group about the accident they have just witnessed.

When you have finished questioning each other, discuss as a class the following points:

- are you impressed (or not) with what you were able to remember?
- do people tend to disagree about what happened?
- does that help you to arrive at what really happened or not?

FOLLOW-UP

You could set up a court scene using one of the 'accidents' as your case. You will need a judge, defending and prosecuting counsel, a jury, a defendant, witnesses and maybe a public gallery. Your teacher will explain what all these people do in a trial – the important thing to remember is that a trial is a very formal occasion and the language used by most people involved will also be formal.

Holiday

If you have done the previous exercise you will have noticed that different people carry different memories away from the same incident. This next piece of drama is based on that idea. Work in groups of three – A, B and C. Your teacher will give you further information.

A and B went on holiday together with B's parents to a small seaside resort. School has just started again and A, B and C have met up at break time. C asks them what they did on holiday.

BULLYING

Bus Stop

CHARACTERS

Robert **Stephen** **Alan** **Rashid**	First formers; they have recently joined the school.
Mr Ellis	The new bus driver; he is also Stephen's uncle.
Graham **Leroy** **Barry**	Third years; they regard the bus as 'theirs'.
Moura **Kim**	

It is early morning and the school bus is nearing the stop where Stephen *and* Robert *get on. The bus is, for once, on time – perhaps because there is a new driver at the wheel.* Moura *and* Kim *are sitting together near the driver gossiping and giggling.* Alan *and* Rashid *are perched on the back seat.*

Stephen   [*climbing up the steps*] Hello, Uncle Bill. Mum said you might be doing this run. I'd better not tell you what else she said though – about how long you'd stick it!

Mr Ellis   Oh aye – she's always been a great believer in my talents has your Mum.

Stephen   This is Rob, me mate. We're in the same class.

Mr Ellis   Hello there Rob. [pause] Well, you'd better get seats you two.

The two boys make their way to back of the bus as it lurches off. They look apprehensively at their friends, who are still sitting on the back seat.

Stephen   Are y' still gonna do it?

Rashid	Yeah. We're not chicken. Not like some I could mention.
Robert	We're not chicken. It just seems daft that's all. You're going to get your head bashed in just so's you can sit on the back seat. You're not brave – you're potty.
Rashid	It's not just so's we can sit on the back seat. It's the . . . the . . . principle of the thing.
Robert	Swallowed a dictionary have you?
Rashid	That's what my Dad said anyway.
Stephen	You told your Dad?
Robert	What did he say? He's not goin' to tell the teachers is he?
Rashid	Come off it – he's not daft. He knows that'd only make things worse. He just said, 'There's some times when you can't let the big mouths push you around; you gotta stand up for yourself – even if you get a thrashing doing it'.
Stephen	Oh.
Alan	Well, you'd better go an' sit with the girls hadn't you? After all, [scornful] we're 'potty' aren't we? You don't want to get mixed up in a nasty scrap do you? Might spoil your pretty clothes.
Robert	[moves to sit on the back seat] Aw, come off it Al. We're your mates aren't we? If you're gonna take on a bunch of yobbos then . . . well . . . we're with you. Right Steve?
Stephen	Um . . . yeah. Right. [nervously] We really are goin' to get a bashing though.
Moura	Hey you lot. You'd better get off that back seat – we're nearly at Barry's stop. He'll murder you if he finds you there after what he said yesterday.
Kim	Well it might keep him occupied for a bit; and off us. My mum didn't half carry on last night when I got home, [mimicking]. 'All afternoon in the cookery class and you come home with a greasy paper doily and a few crumbs.' Greedy pig; he pinched the lot.
	The bus pulls to a halt. Barry, Graham and Leroy come noisily up the steps. They are dressed in school uniform – but only just. Nearly every item is calculated to offend; school ties barely recognisable except by their colour, trousers of regulation colour but fashionable cut etc. They fail to notice that they have a new bus driver.
Barry	[stopping by the two girls] Eh! Them cakes went down a treat last night. When you doin' cooking again?
Moura	[risking bravery] I'm not likely to tell you am I? Pig!

Barry	Hey! Wait a minute, did you 'ear that fellas? Miss Charmin' 'ere says I'm a pig.
Graham	That's nothing to what you're goin' to say when you see what company we've got this morning. Come 'ere Barry . . . there's a row of midget seat nickers at the back here.
Leroy	[*leaning over the now silent and terrified first formers on the back row*] I think you lot o' dwarfs 'ad better move. This is OUR seat.
Robert	[*quavering*] No it's not. You can't reserve seats on a school bus.
Barry	Is that so? You're about to find out just how wrong you can be sometimes.
Leroy	'Ang on Barry. I've got a better idea. [*He grins knowingly at* Barry *and* Graham]. These lot look as if they could do with some company, don't they? You know, someone to cheer their miserable little lives up – even warm 'em up. Know what I mean?
Barry	[*catching on*] Yeah . . . maybe you got summat there Leroy . . . and well . . . they did come looking for our company now . . . didn't they?
	[Graham *and* Leroy *sit on either side of the four first form boys while* Barry *effectively blocks their escape route by sprawling over two seats and spanning the aisle. Their prey thus cornered, they pull out cigarettes and light up.*]
Barry	[*blowing smoke in the faces of the small boys*] Eh girls, you're keen on cookery aren't you? Come and 'ave a look at this then. I've invented a new dish – kippered first year!
Moura	Someone should report you lot. Leave them alone, they're doing no harm. You just like picking on kids that can't fight back.
Barry	Who rattled your cage this morning eh? What I do is my business – and if any la-di-da teacher gets to know about this, I'll know who to come an' look for, won't I?
Graham	You tell her, Barry.
Leroy	Hey come on, we'll be at school before we've 'ad a chance to get to know our little pals 'ere. Hey you, [*he pushes* Robert *on the chest*] you were the big brave one a minute ago, how d'y fancy a fag eh?
Robert	I don't smoke. It's stupid; and anyway you're not allowed to smoke on the bus.
Leroy	[*mimics* Robert] 'Oh I don't smoke thank you' . . . well you're gonna try it this morning, isn't he lads?
Graham	Yeah. Here Leroy, 'ave this one. [*He hands a lit cigarette to* Leroy.]

Leroy	Right then; put this in yer mouth and suck hard.
Stephen	Leave him alone.
Rashid	You'll make him sick if you do that.
Graham	Yeah, that's right; it'll make him sick.
Robert	No it won't. You can't make me smoke a cigarette if I don't want to.
Barry	Oh dear . . . 'e 'as got a lot to learn, hasn't he? [*He leans over and grabs Stephen, expertly pinning his arms behind him.*] Now then, either you smoke that fag or your mate here gets thumped. D'you get it?

FOLLOW-UP

What do you think would happen now?
Improvise the final scene of the play.

Quickies

You listen to me

Work with a partner. Both of you must try to talk the other person 'down' without stopping or being interrupted. Begin when the teacher gives the signal.

Odd one out

You will need to work in groups of four or five. One person is totally ignored while the rest of the group play a game or chat amongst themselves. Everyone in the group should take a turn at being the 'odd one out'. Try as many ways as possible to get the rest of the group to notice you.

Threats

Work with a partner – A and B. A meets B on the way to school and demands his/her dinner money. A may make threats about what will happen to B if the money is not handed over, but may not touch B at all. Change places after two or three minutes.

Crowds

Move around at random and when the teacher gives a signal begin to talk to the nearest person. Complain, moan, insult and generally be unpleasant to them. Stop when the teacher gives a signal and move off again. At the next signal, tell the person nearest to you what you like about them – it must be genuine and you must mention at least one thing.

Fantasy

Work in pairs. Imagine that you are now 20 years old and have left school. Your partner is the teacher whom you have most disliked while at school. You now have the opportunity to say all the things you always wanted to say to them!

Now imagine that your partner is the teacher you liked, admired or respected while at school. Tell them why you liked them.

Trust me

Work with a partner – A and B. A lies on the floor. B takes A's head in his/her hands and supports it completely (you will find it easier if you kneel behind your partner with your knees on either side of their head). A tries to relax the neck muscles while B rolls the head very slowly from side to side.

Although this sounds simple it is very, very difficult to do! You have to be able to trust your partner absolutely.

Discussion

Bullying is often a sensitive subject. Discuss the following points in small groups:
- what does it feel like to be bullied?
- what does it feel like to bully someone else?
- in the 'odd one out' exercise did anyone manage to force the group to notice them? How?
- in 'Threats' was there anyone who resisted the bully? How?
- why are some people bullies?
- are there any ways of changing them?
- is it easier to think of insults for other people than compliments?
- which do you prefer to receive?
- how did you feel in 'Fantasy'?

Starting Points

Sentence starters

Work together in groups. Each group is given one of the sentences below to use as a starter for a timed improvisation. One of the characters in the group must use the sentence as either the opening, or the closing, line of the play.

Why can't you get home on time?

You're always picking on me.

You'll have to learn to stick up for yourself.

I've been hearing things about you.

He's coming now!

You're too big for your boots.

If you don't leave me alone I'll . . .

Who's telling the truth? (role play)

Work in groups of four. Each person takes one of the following characters:

Head teacher
Pupil A
Pupil B
Mrs Saunders

SITUATION

Two pupils, A and B, have been called to the Head teacher's office after they have been caught fighting in the playground. Half way through the interview Mrs Saunders is shown into the room. Your teacher will give you further information.

FOLLOW-UP

Improvise the scene at either pupil's house that evening when school is over.

Mrs Saunders meets the parents of either A or B in the street. What would be said?

Factory

You are workers in the packaging department of a large confectionery factory. Your job is to make star-shaped paper containers to hold sweets. You will be given square sheets of paper. Follow the instructions below to make the containers.

You work in groups of about six or seven people. You are paid by the number of containers you make during each session; every so often a foreman will collect your containers and make a note of how many you have done – he will then pay you for the work you have completed.

Most of the people in your group have worked at the factory for about two years so you all know each other very well. You spend a lot of your time talking, gossiping and cracking jokes – it slows the work down and means that you don't earn quite as much money as you could, but you prefer it this way.

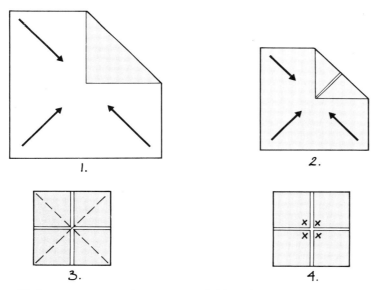

1. Fold each corner into the middle of the square.
2. Turn the paper over and turn each corner into the middle.
3. Turn the paper over again and fold along dotted lines.
4. Lift each flap at X and pull outwards to complete your container.

Who's next?

Work in groups of three. A is the owner of a fruit and vegetable stall, B is a rather timid person and C is you as you are.

You are in the market. B is being served and has asked for a pound of tomatoes. There are some nice firm ones at the front of the display, but A would like to get rid of the rather bruised ones at the back. B doesn't look the kind of person to make a fuss. There are a lot of other people waiting to be served and C is in a hurry.

What do you think would happen? Remember that C must behave as you really would in this situation. Swop over until all three have played the part of C.

Too cold

Work in groups of about eight – six prisoners and two guards. You are in a labour camp in the far north of a very cold country. Your job is to build a wall. To do this you will have to mix cement, carry the cement to the wall, carry the bricks, lay the bricks and make sure that they are laid straight. This would not be too difficult except that the temperature is minus ten degrees celcius. At this temperature you have to mix cement near the fire and when you lay the bricks they will freeze solidly in position, so you must be careful to make no mistakes.

You must try to keep warm. The only way to do this is either to stay near the fire or to work hard enough to sweat, but you are weak and cold and badly fed.

The guards are just about to lead you out to start work. The main thought in all the prisoners' heads is that at the end of this work session they will be fed – with hot soup!

TELLING STORIES

Making Prince Dougie Laugh

CHARACTERS

The King	[Fenton] A comfortable sort of man, but fed up with his miserable son.
The Queen	[Claudia] An extremely dignified lady.
Prince Dougie	Only son of the King and Queen. Surly and not too bright. He hasn't laughed for ten years.
Jester	Came to the court ten years ago. The Prince has never even smiled at one of his jokes.
Lil	Barmaid; loud and a bit pushy.
Jessy	Barmaid; louder and pushier.
Horse	Permanently tired, and not above a little trickery to get his own way.
Man	Well meaning; makes the mistake of thinking Horse is the same.
Mrs Topps	Eighty years old.
Homer Topps	Her son.
Joe Topps	Her brother.
Mr Elton and Mrs Elton	Neighbours.
Doctor	
Janice	Assistant at the mortuary.
Priest	
Two policemen	
Two guards	
Gloria	

SCENE ONE

The Queen *is sitting on her throne. The* Jester *is trying to amuse her but without success. The* King *enters reading a letter and looking worried.*

King [*flapping a letter about*] Look! Another one. That makes three this week.

Queen Fenton darling, 'That makes three this week', do you know that makes no sense at all? You railly must learn to speak properly. You cannot be the king and continue to speak like a common working man – you have your position to think of. I know of what I am talking; why, my deah fahther would . . .

King Claudia, belt up – this needs looking at. This [*waves the letter at her*], came from the father of Her Highness the Worshipful Princess Sophia of Salubria. Her royal dad says that he has no wish to condemn his daughter to a life of certain misery. After meeting our highly intelligent and charming son last week he has decided the wedding is off!

Jester Ding-dong . . . no wedding bells . . . Sophia thinks that Dougie sm . . . ! Sorry! No offence meant your ladyship. [Prince Dougie *approaches*] Don't fall about now but sunshine boy is coming this way.

King And she was the last of them. I've asked every single princess in the book if they want to marry our Dougie – even the ugly ones said no thanks.
[*He looks across at* Dougie, *who is sitting with his head in his hands. He looks utterly miserable.*]
Mind you, can't say I blame them. I mean look at him, who'd want to live with that wet weekend? If only he'd cheer up a bit – crack his face just once.

Jester [*to audience*] Hopeless case you see. Even when his mother fell off her horse and landed on her backside in the mud, all he did was grunt and go home for his tea. No offence meant your ladyship.

Queen Really! You should do something about him Fenton.

King Yes I know. But what?

Queen Sack him of course – he's impertinent!

King Sack Dougie? What an odd idea. I can't do that my love.

Queen Not Dougie – idiot! The jester.

King Oh I couldn't do that sweetheart. He's the only person who laughs at my jokes. But I must do something about it. Surely someone would have him. I mean, he owns a very nice little palace . . . and two breweries.

Jester Then you'd better ask the barmaids if they'll have him.

[*The* King *stares at him; then grabs him by the arms and dances him round.*]

King	Of course! Why didn't I think of that! I knew you'd earn your keep some day! We'll have a competition. The first person – well girl then – who can make Dougie laugh can have the breweries . . . as long as she marries Dougie.
Jester	Eh, not bad, King. Not bad at all.
Queen	Imagine – a common barmaid for a daughter-in-law! Fenton, if you go ahead with this dreadful idea I shall never speak to you again!
Jester	That probably settles it then.

SCENE TWO

At the palace. The King *has announced his competition. He and the* Queen *are sitting in the throne room waiting for the first contestant. The* King *is restless and expectant while the* Queen *sits in frozen dignity. Prince Dougie is, as usual, thoroughly miserable. There are two Guards by the door. Behind them is a crowd of people.*

King	Send in the first contestant.
Queen	The King says send in the first contestant.
Jester	The King says send in the first contestant.
Guard 1	The King says send in the first contestant.
Guard 2	Send in the first contestant! I wish she wouldn't keep doing that – I can hear him.
Lil	[*Pushing to the front of the line*] C'mon dearie, that's me. I was 'ere first. [*Turns to the rest of the crowd.*] You might as well all go 'ome now me loves – I've got this little lot all wrapped up.
Jessy	Oo d'you think you are? Reckon you're better than us do you?
Lil	Just you hang around then dearie – I'll 'ave 'im laughing till he hurts! [*The* guards *escort her to the* King *and* Queen.]
King	Well now m' dear. Think you can . . .
Queen	Begin! [*She points a finger imperiously and glares icily at the unfortunate* Lil *who now begins to stammer through her story.*]
Lil	Oh. Er . . . yes your ladysh . . . highness. My story starts in the . . . er . . . countryside . . . with a man . . . who . . . er . . . has this cart . . . see . . . and he. . . . [*She pauses, looks at the* King, *who nods encouragingly at her; she continues more confidently.*] Cabbages. See? He had more cabbages than he knew what to do with so he was taking a load of them to sell in the local market.
	[*At this point the* Man *and the* Horse *begin to act out the story on the front of the stage, while* Lil *in the background mimes her narration. During this scene* Horse *always speaks directly to the audience.*]

Man	Git going Horse. [*He cracks the whip.*] If youse eyes weren't open I'd swear youse was asleep.
Horse	That's no way to speak to a dumb animal. I'm fed up with this – dragging me out of my stable. I'll have the RSPCA on him ... with his 'git going' and his whip.
Man	Giddy up Horse. [*Cracks whip again.*]
Horse	[*in disgust*] 'Giddy up'! Good grief, the man hasn't got a brain in his head. Well that does it, I'm not going a step further. [*He stops.*]
Man	Hey! C'mon Horse. You can't stop there. We've got to get to market this morning.
Horse	I like that! There's only one person round here who has to get to market – and it's not me.
Man	[*inspecting* Horse *closely*] I know what it is – cart's too heavy isn't it? Poor ol' faithful Horse. You're nuthin' but a bag of old bones – just like me.
Horse	Just like you? I beg to differ with you there. At least I've still got all my own teeth.
Man	Tell you what . . . I'll take a couple of these cabbages off the back . . . make it a bit easier for you. [*Takes two large cabbages off the cart.*] How's that then?
Horse	Nice, very nice. How about a few more while you're at it?
Man	C'mon now Horse – get a move on.
Horse	Not likely. I'm stopping right here.
Man	I s'pose I'd better make the load even lighter. Horse is really getting past it. [*He unloads even more cabbages.*] How's about that then?
Horse	Pardon? You spoke? I suppose I might just amble along a bit; there's a very fine view from that turn in the road. [*He pulls the cart for a few feet and then stops again.*]
Man	We'll never get to the market like this. [*He uses his whip again.*] Git movin' you idle beast.
Horse	I knew we'd come to this – insults! That does it, not another step!
Man	C'mon, there's only one thing to do with you. [*The Man takes all the remaining cabbages off the cart, and staggers off down the road towards the market followed by the triumphant Horse.*]
Horse	Now this is what I call an acceptable division of labour!
	[Horse *and* Man *exit.*]
King	Bravo! A fine story. Didn't you think so Dougie?

Dougie	[*looks up*] Mm? What story? I didn't notice anything.
King	What do you mean 'what story'? Weren't you listening? [*Turns to the Queen.*] Some fine manners you've taught this son of yours I must say.
Queen	His manners have absolutely nothing to do with my side of the family. I have to say, though, that I am often strongly reminded of your Uncle Samuel.
Lil	It's alright your 'ighness. I'm not really sorry I couldn't make 'im laugh. I mean, it would be very nice to own a couple of breweries and live in a palace, but well, I'm not cut out to be married to someone who doesn't like a good laugh now and then. I like to have a bit of fun.
Jester	And Prince Dougie isn't exactly a barrel of laughs. Right?
Lil	Right!
	[Jessy *pushes her way past the guards. She approaches the* King *and* Queen.]
Jessy	How about someone else havin' a go? Someone who knows a bit about it? There's been men come into my bar, men who've lost their jobs . . . or their wives . . . or their money. Those men have gone home with a smile on their faces after a couple of drinks and some of my stories.
King	Well Madam, you're very welcome to try, but I'm beginning to think it's hopeless.
Jessy	Just you wait. Are you listening Dougie? [Dougie *gives no indication that he has heard.*] That's okay. I've seen that before too – looks like they couldn't care less but inside they is listening real hard. We start upstairs in the bedroom. An old woman lies on the bed; she is dying. Her son is beside her listening to her last words . . .
	[*As with the previous story the action is now taken up on the front of the stage by* Homer, *the son, and* Mrs Topps, *his mother. The bedcovers of* Mrs Topps' *bed are littered with papers; insurance policies, mortage deeds, etc.*]
Mrs Topps	It's all yours son – every last penny. Look after yourself when I'm gone and don't let that thieving brother of mine get his hands on a penny. Make sure you . . . look after. . . . Sensible (*she dies*].
Homer	Have you gone then Mother? [*He shakes her.*] You're not going to wake up again like you did last week? Nope, you've gone for good this time. [*He picks up the papers as* Joe Topps *enters*]
Joe	Poor old girl. Perhaps she'll get a bit of peace now. What's she left you?
Homer	Everything. Sounds grand don't it? What it means is just enough money to pay off her debts. And of course I've got Sensible, the pig. He'd be worth a bit in bacon, except for her will. He's to be allowed to spend his 'declining years in happiness and tranquility' – at my expense! There isn't even enough money for a decent funeral.

Joe	Aren't you supposed to get hold of a doctor now?
Homer	What for? Any fool can see she's dead.
Joe	To sign that she is.
Homer	Oh . . . I hadn't thought of that. We'd better get down to the surgery then. Help me get her dressed.

[*Together they dress the corpse in her going out clothes – coat, gloves, hat and handbag. It takes them some time because* Mrs Topps *is quite stiff by now.*]

Joe	There, she looks a treat. Give me a hand with her down the stairs. What time's the next bus?
Homer	Half past. We can make it.

[Joe *and* Homer, *with* Mrs Topps *held rigidly between them, move towards a bus queue which has formed on the other side of the stage. They prop her up against a lamp post when they get there.*]

Mr Elton	Good morning madam. I'm glad to see you up and about again. Heard you were quite poorly. [*He raises his hat.*]
Mrs Elton	Yes indeed Mrs Topps, we were all worried about you [*nods of agreement from the rest of the bus queue*]. Will you be down at the club this afternoon then? We've got the bingo on. You always did like that.
Homer	I'm sorry but my mother is . . . is . . . she's got to see the doctor today.
Mrs Elton	Well thank you young man, but I'm sure your mother can speak for herself.
Homer	She can't . . . you see . . . she's . . . she's . . . not quite with us at the moment. If you see what I mean.
Mr Elton	[*apologetic*] Terribly sorry . . . didn't think . . . must have been the strain of her illness or something? Nervous breakdown . . . terrible thing . . . chap I knew once . . . completely off his rocker . . . dreadful.
Joe	I think we'd better go.

[*They arrive at the* doctor's *surgery.*]

Doctor	Come in . . . come in. Now, what seems to be the matter?
Homer	It's my mother, doctor. She's dead.
Doctor	Yes, well perhaps you could just leave the diagnosis to me. What are her symptoms?
Homer	She hasn't got any.

Doctor	What d'you mean? If she's ill she must have symptoms. Perhaps I'd better just have a look at her. Hmm . . . she doesn't look very well does she? [*He feels her pulse and listens to her heart with mounting panic.*] This woman is dead! What is she doing here?
Joe	[*patiently*] We wanted you to write a death certificate.
Doctor	Oh you did, did you? So you calmly walk in here lugging a corpse with you? You must be off your heads. She should be on ice down in the mortuary.
Homer	Okay. We'll take her there then. Thanks for your trouble.

[Joe *and* Homer *exit still carrying* Mrs Topps.]

Doctor	No wait! You can't go on the streets with that . . . that . . . body [*pause, then speaks into his intercom*]. Send in the next patient please nurse. And nurse . . . just check they're still alive before they come in here.

[Homer *and* Joe *put* Mrs Topps *against the wall and ring the bell outside the hospital mortuary. A brisk young woman,* Janice, *answers.*]

Janice	Can I help you?
Homer	Yes. Can I book my mother in?
Janice	I'm sorry, I don't quite follow you.
Joe	His mother. [*He indicates* Mrs Topps *leaning against the wall.*] He wants to put her on ice. This is where you put dead people isn't it?
Janice	Yes, but . . . this is most irregular. They are usually delivered properly . . . not just . . . well . . . carried here. And you haven't got any of the proper forms with you. How can I deal with this without any forms?
Homer	We'll sign the forms. We don't mind.
Janice	Would you? That would be a great help. Now let me see, you should have a B160 and two copies of T225 . . . then you'll need a Cadaver Transit Permit . . . an Accidental Damage Waiver . . .
Joe	Accidental Damage? She's not staying here if that's the picture. Being dead's bad enough . . . she don't have to get damaged as well. Come on Homer – looks like we'll have to do this ourselves.

[Homer *and* Joe *are in the graveyard. They are digging a large hole.* Mrs Topps *has been laid nearby on a convenient tomb.*]

Homer	Do graves have to be six foot deep, Joe?
Joe	Just dig, Homer.
Homer	Why six foot? Why not seven, or five and a half?
Joe	Just dig, Homer.

[*Meanwhile, a priest* has spotted the two men digging in the graveyard and *has come to his own dreadful conclusion. He is on the phone to the police.*]

Priest Yes Sergeant . . . just two of them . . . digging up the remains of the dear departed . . . may God have mercy on their souls. Holy Mother of God, they must be in the devil's grip.

[*Moments later the sound of the police siren is heard. The* priest *is joined by two policemen. All three make their way across the graveyard towards* Homer *and* Joe.]

Homer Look! Something must be going on.

Joe It's us what's going on, you dope! They think we're vampires or something. Come on, we'd better get out of here.

[*They drop their spades and run off. At this point* Mrs Topps *sits up.*]

Mrs Topps Never get any peace. You'd think once you was dead they'd leave you alone . . . dragged all over town . . . insulted [*she adjusts her hat*] . . . and now I can't even get buried in peace. I'd better find Sensible before that Joe turns him into pork sausages.

[*She marches off in a thoroughly bad temper. At the back of the stage* Gloria *enters. She sits beside* Dougie *and begins to talk to him quietly. It soon becomes apparent that he is interested in what she is saying.*]

King That was very good. Excellent, m'dear. Didn't you think so Claudia?

Queen Don't speak to me. I think the whole thing is in extremely poor taste.

Jester Look!

[*The whole court sees* Dougie *smile. The smile is followed by a grin; the grin by a chuckle. Then* Dougie *begins to laugh. He shrieks, chortles, bellows and rolls on the floor. Finally he stands up and leads* Gloria *over to the* King *and* Queen.]

Dougie Sire. Madam. Meet Gloria. I'm going to marry her.

King Um . . . er . . . yes well, I suppose that's in order . . . er, don't you think my love?

Queen I think it's all competely ridiculous. Excuse me, I feel a headache coming on.

King Well that's that then. You have my permission of course. [*He turns to the* Jester.] There's just one thing I'd like to know. How did she do it? She must be a genius.

Jester Not a genius, Sire . . . she just happens to be my sister you see . . . and there's always been talent in our family.

Quickies

When . . . where . . . what

Each person has three pieces of paper. Write down the name of a character, a place and an object. You can use either real places and people (for example, a famous actor or pop star), or you can describe them (for example, an irritable old man or a bored child).

Put the pieces of paper into three piles and shuffle them well. Break into groups of between three and five. Each group takes a piece of paper from each pile, and then creates a story based around the character, place and object on the pieces of paper.

Circle stories

This exercise uses 'word association'. This is what happens when you hear one word and it reminds you of another. So the word 'rat' might lead you on to: grey, evil, cunning, secret, sharp etc. There are various different word association games.

a) One person in the circle starts off with a word – it might be something very simple like 'red'. The next person says, 'Red reminds me of traffic lights'. The following person says, 'Traffic lights remind me of fumes'. Carry on round the circle. Sometimes if you get an interesting sequence of words they can be turned into a story.
b) Again you start with one word but this time each person adds a word that will make sense – you are making a sentence. A group of ten people might end up with 'The man with a bandaged leg crawled into the shelter'.

c) This time everyone adds a phrase of several words or a sentence, as you go round the circle. Don't forget that you are trying to create a story, so each sentence should follow on from the previous one. Improvise your story when you are satisfied with the result.

1001 uses for . . .

Work in groups of six to eight. Choose one of the objects from the list below and think of as many uses for it as you can (you don't have to limit yourselves to the ordinary uses of the object you choose – a bottle can hold milk, but it could also carry a message if you were stuck on a desert island):
- blanket
- nail
- brick
- lipstick
- bag of frozen peas
- tennis racquet
- plastic carrier bag
- bicycle inner tube.

This thingummyjig

Sit together in a circle. In the centre there is a collection of objects. Close your eyes, lean forward and choose one of the objects. Invent a story which involves your object in some way. Go round the circle telling your stories.

Starting Points

Not only but also

Many poems, songs and nursery rhymes tell stories as shortened versions. If you think about it, there are probably many more characters in the background of these well known songs and verses. Take for example 'Pussy in the well':

> *Ding, dong bell*
> *Pussy's down the well*
> *Who put him in?*
> *Little Tommy Thin*
> *Who pulled him out?*
> *Little Tommy Stout.*

- who did Pussy belong to?
- had Pussy done anything to deserve such treatment or was Tommy Thin just a cruel boy?
- how did Pussy's owner feel about all this?
- was Tommy thin?
- why? Didn't his parents feed him?
- who were his parents? Did he have any?
- were people pleased with Tommy Stout for rescuing the cat?
- what might they have done to show they were pleased?
- does Tommy Stout have many friends?
- who are they?

If you answered all the questions you will have now built up a much more detailed picture of 'Pussy in the Well'.

Choose a song, nursery rhyme or poem. Make sure that everyone in your group knows the words. Now build up the details in the background, by asking questions like those for 'Pussy in the Well'. When the whole group is happy with what has been produced, improvise your version.

Cartoon

Cartoon films, such as Walt Disney films, are made up of a series of separate drawings, called 'frames'. When they are run together very quickly, the characters look as though they are moving.

Work in groups of six or seven. Choose one of the movements from the list below (or decide on your own) and decide how many separate frames you would need, to show the movement on film. Each person in the group takes a frame, which will be one small part of the entire movement.

Now you have to try to run the frames one after another so that the whole movement is clear (it's not easy to get the timing right – it helps if one person acts as the director):
- hammering in a nail
- picking up a kitten (don't use a real one!)
- sneezing
- a rather snooty person picking up a smelly sock
- batting at cricket
- drinking a fizzy drink.

WORDS

Say That Again?

CHARACTERS

Gary	Isobel	Brian
Thomas	Mary	Glyn
Eddie	Nani	
	Tracey	

A new girl, Mary, has just started in the school. She has strange powers – she can make words come to life.

Thomas   Hey Nani, give us your maths homework; didn't have time to do it last night did I.

Nani   You never do.

Thomas   What d'you mean by that?

Isobel   She means you never do your own work; you always copy other people's.

Eddie   Oooh! Listen to Miss – p'raps you'd better mind your own business.

Isobel   It is my business – Nani's my friend.

Gary   And Tom's mine. I look after his interests you might say . . . [*He grabs the maths book from* Nani.] Here y'are Tom – help yourself.

Tracey   I suppose it's the only way he'll ever get any of them right.

Thomas   You watch your mouth girl. I'm not thick – just got better things to do with my time that's all.

Brian   Better things? D'you mean like getting one of your mates to pinch a girl's book? Can't you even do that yourself?

Thomas   There's one thing I can do. I can shut you up, no trouble.

Brian   And there's no doubt about how you'd do that is there?

Thomas	Right again brainbox. Is this what you meant?
	[*He aims a fierce punch at* Brian *which catches him in the stomach and leaves him gasping. While* Glyn *and the girls gather round* Brian, Thomas *and his friends move away.* Mary, *who has been watching the incident, now approaches the group.*]
Mary	Excuse me. I couldn't help hearing all that . . . can I help?
Glyn	You're new here aren't you? You'll have to get used to that mob – they're always like that. If you don't do what they want they thump you.
Tracey	And before you say it, it's no good going to the teachers. They never see it happening – Tom and his mates are too clever for that.
Nani	I just wish there was some way of getting them, but hitting people is all they understand.
Mary	You could use words.
Brian	Words? Are you potty? Words wouldn't hurt them!
Mary	My words would.
Brian	What are you on about?
Mary	Words . . . I can make them real.
Isobel	Come off it Mary . . . that's dreamtime stuff.
Mary	Pinch!
Isobel	Ow! Who did that? Someone pinched my arm really hard!
Mary	It was me.
Glyn	But you never even touched her!
Mary	Fog!
Brian	Hey! Where's everyone?
Tracey	I can't see anything!
Glyn	[*gropes blindly forward*] Mary? Did you do that?
Mary	Of course I did stupid. How else could it have happened?
Glyn	I could be having a nightmare? Can you make it go away then?
Mary	Easy! . . . Clear!
Nani	I just don't believe it. Things like that don't happen do they? Can you do one to me? Not a nasty one though!
Mary	Um . . . how about . . . warm!
Nani	Oooh! That's lovely. I feel like . . . like I'm near the fire, wrapped up in my quilt, eating hot toast – all at the same time!

Isobel	You can use words then; and you could use words on Tom and his horrible crowd.
Mary	Hmm . . . I don't know really. It seems a bit unfair.
Brian	Unfair! You try one of his punches then for a bit of unfair!
Tracey	You'd better make your mind up quick. They're coming back for round two.

[Thomas, Gary *and* Eddie *come back into the classroom.*]

Thomas	Here y'are Nani banani [*throws Nani's* maths book which lands on the floor].
Brian	Pick it up. Yes you, you great moron. You dropped her book. Pick it up!
Thomas	[*he can hardly believe what he is hearing*] You what? Aren't you the kid who had a belly full of fist about five minutes ago?
Brian	Yep, that's me – got a bad memory have you? No wonder you find the maths too difficult.
Thomas	Whaaat! You cheeky kid. Gary . . . Eddie . . . get 'im.
Mary	I wouldn't do that if I were you.
Gary	Why not? It's a good laugh.
Mary	Well I wouldn't like you to get hurt.
Eddie	Thank you kind lady [*he makes a mock bow*], but we're not the ones who'll get hurt.
Mary	Hot!

[Eddie *trys to grab* Brian *but as soon as he touches him he reacts as if he were burning hot.*]

Eddie	Ow! My hand! [*He sucks his fingers desperately.*]
Gary	What are you up to eh? Trying funny stuff?
Mary	Dizzy!
Gary	Ed . . . oh . . . I feel all . . . all [*he slithers to the floor in an untidy heap*].
Thomas	Here . . . what's going on? What are you doing?
Mary	Only saying words. How about one for you? Something suitable I think . . . donkey!
Thomas	Eee Aaw, Eee Aaw
Isobel	I'm going to wake up in a minute, I know I am. Things like this don't happen. [*pause*] Mary, is he going to stay like that?

Mary	Oh no, it usually wears off after a couple of minutes. It's not real you know; well only for a bit.
Isobel	Can you do other things with it? I mean could you make nasty people be nice for a bit? If they got used to it they might stay that way.
Mary	I've only ever tried that once. My Mum always used to complain about how much Dad snored at night, so for about three nights I used words to keep him quiet.
Glyn	And did he stop?
Mary	I don't know – Mum didn't sleep for three nights because it was so quiet, so I gave up.
Tracey	I don't know whether any of you are interested, but these three seem to be taking their time about coming round.
	[*She is right. The three boys are still suffering the effects of the words* Mary *used on them.*]
Mary	Oh dear. This is getting a bit out of hand. What happens if they stay like that?
Brian	We'll all have some explaining to do; and can you imagine it? I can just see the Head believing this!
Tracey	I think it's all right. Gary opened an eye just then – I think it's wearing off.
	[*The friends move away and watch from a distance.*]
Gary	[*sits up groggily*] Uuh? What happened? . . . Oh my head!
Eddie	It was that kid. He must have knocked you out.
Gary	Don't be daft. Not a little kid like that. My head doesn't half hurt though.
Eddie	And my hands must be blistered. They felt burnt right through. Ask Tom about the kid.
Gary	Hey Tom . . . what did that kid do?
Thomas	Eee Aaw, Eee Aaw.
Gary	Stop mucking around Tom. This isn't a joke.
Thomas	I Eee know. Eee Aaw . . . can't speeeek Eee Aaw
Gary	Oh my god! He's off his rocker.
	[*In the distance a school bell rings.*]
Mary	They'll be okay. It's wearing off quite fast now. I just wish I was in Tom's class; I'd love to be there when the teacher calls the class register and Tom has to answer his name!

Quickies

Chinese whispers

Sit together in a circle. One person whispers a sentence or phrase to the person beside them. The sentence is passed on in whispers around the circle. The last person speaks the sentence out loud. In nearly every case the final sentence will be completely different.

American Indian names

a) Work in pairs. Choose an American Indian type of name for yourself and work out a sign to go with it. (For example, Running Deer could be shown by miming running, and holding your hands (spread out) on your head to indicate a deer's antlers.) Your partner has to guess your name from the sign.

b) Sit together in a circle. Everyone in turn mimes their American Indian names. One person starts by miming his or her own name, together with someone else's. The other person must respond immediately by miming his or her name, plus another person's. Anyone who does not respond to their sign or who cannot demonstrate another's must drop out.

Spell

Work in pairs. A wicked witch has stolen all the words you know – except four. Using the four words you have chosen to keep (and by making gestures), communicate an idea to your partner. It can be any idea you like, from a warning about a fire in the building to a comment about the weather, but your partner must understand your message.

When your ideas have been exchanged you can use each other's words, giving you a total of eight words. Move on to a new partner and exchange another idea. Again you can use each other's words – you should now have a total of sixteen. Carry on until you run out of people, ideas or words.

Alphabet

Working in two teams, you are going to use your bodies to form the shape of the letters of the alphabet. Some letters may need two people. Obviously you can't hope to do all 26 letters, so try to choose those which you think are most commonly used.

Your teacher will call out a word and the first team to form it using themselves for the letters will be the winners.

Extension. Develop shapes to represent commas, full stops, exclamation marks and question marks. The first team to build a whole sentence will be the winners.

Opposites

Work with a partner – A and B. When A says a word B must respond with its opposite. For example:
sad/happy
wet/dry
smart/shabby

Adverbs

Sit together in a circle. One person is chosen to go out of the room, while the rest agree on an adverb. When the outsider returns, he or she tries to find out what the word is by asking the others to mime an action in the way of the adverb. For example he could ask someone to dance 'in this way'. If the adverb was 'sadly', the dance would be a very mournful one. The outsider may ask for three mimes to help him guess the word. If he cannot guess the word he or she must drop out until the end of the game.

Starting Points

Sentence starters

The way in which we use words is noticed constantly by other people. Try using some of the following sentences in short improvised scenes.

Did you hear what he said to me?

Say it properly then.

I knew what he was like the moment he opened his mouth.

I beg your pardon!

Well, what do you say to that then?

What's he on about?

I merely remarked . . .

Mind your language

Working in small groups, invent nonsense words to describe the ordinary things around you. Don't forget your own bodies; you can make up words for hair, hands, feet etc. Practise using these words until everyone is familiar with them. Then, one person from each group moves on to another group. Each 'stranger' must try to explain something to the people in the new group – he could be lost, hungry, need to know the time, or anything else he chooses. However, neither party may use any language other than the nonsense words which have been developed.

Is it a good fit?

We all use different kinds of language in different situations. For example, you probably don't talk to your headteacher and your friend in the same way. This piece of work asks you to use language that would be most *appropriate* for the situation.

Work in small groups. Quickly improvise scenes on the situations below – pay particular attention to the language you use.

a) Members of a stone-age tribe are engaged in various tasks. Some are picking berries, some are skinning an animal, some are chipping flints to make arrow and axe heads. One of the flint chippers makes a spark which falls on to some dry grass and sets it alight: fire is discovered.

b) Two elderly men working on an allotment, discover that their carefully tended prize strawberry patches have been raided – not one ripe strawberry remains. They strongly suspect the children from the local estate.

c) A thirteen year old girl wants to borrow some of her older brother's cassette tapes to take to a party. They don't normally get on very well together.

d) The same girl tells one of her friends what happened when she asked her brother for the tapes.

e) A court scene in the seventeenth century. A scientist is trying to explain to the king and queen how his new invention works. He has invented the telescope.

SCHOOL RULES

Breaking the Rules

CHARACTERS

Rani	
Karen	
Aaron	3rd year pupils
Sam	
Miss Yates	Karen's form teacher
Mr Ferguson	Maths teacher
Headteacher	
Karl	1st year pupil

SCENE ONE

Four pupils are in an otherwise empty classroom. The teacher's cupboard has been left open and one of the pupils has discovered a box full of new pens, pencils, rubbers, etc

Rani   Hey! Look what I've found!

Aaron   Just what I need. Old Watkins is bound to give me earache next lesson if I haven't got a pen again – which I haven't.

Karen   Don't they look nice. All in their boxes, and not chewed up or nothing.

Rani   Go on . . . take some. Go on . . . they won't bite you.

Karen   Don't be daft. They're bound to find out if some of these go missing.

Aaron   You're like an old woman you are – don't do this, don't do that. What are you scared of? Afraid the big bad teacher will catch you?

Sam   You don't have to worry about getting caught. We do this all the time – never been done yet have we? All you do is take a pile of stuff and what you don't want, you flog to first years.

Karen   For money?

38

Sam	[*sarcastically*] Naa . . . give 'em away don't we?
Karen	There's a lot of them boxes in there. They'll not miss a few pens [*She takes a handful of pens.*] Here, stick these in your pocket for me.
Sam	God! Listen to the master criminal talking. A minute ago she'd have run a mile!
Rani	Shut up Sam. Just take the stuff and get out.

SCENE TWO

Miss Yates *and* Mr Ferguson *approach the classroom.*

Miss Yates	Karen Woods is in your class isn't she?
Mr Ferguson	Yes. Why?
Miss Yates	Would you keep an eye on her for me? I think she may be needing some help but I'm not sure yet.
Mr Ferguson	What do you mean?
Miss Yates	I met her Mum yesterday when I popped out to the shops. She told me that Mr Woods had come back home about ten days ago. Mind you, I would have guessed that anyway – she had a real shiner of a black eye.
Mr Ferguson	And you think he might start on Karen?
Miss Yates	I'm afraid so. She won't tell you though. Last time it happened he broke one of her ribs. It was just luck that we had a medical inspection that day and the doctor spotted it.
Mr Ferguson	So what do I do?
Miss Yates	Not a lot you can do really, except to watch out for obvious signs. You know; bruises, cuts, that sort of thing.
Mr Ferguson	Poor kid. It's a lot to cope with isn't it?
Miss Yates	She doesn't cope with it – just puts up with it. There is a difference.
Mr Ferguson	I might as well get you those folders you wanted while you're down here. I put them at the back of my cupboard. [*He reaches into the cupboard.*] That's odd, I thought I'd put a new box in here.
Miss Yates	What's odd?
Mr Ferguson	A box of new pens. They were here ten minutes ago, I'm sure of it; that'll be the second lot that's gone missing this week. I'd better see the Head about it I suppose. If it doesn't get stopped it snowballs. You get kids who wouldn't dream of stealing things nicking stuff all over the place. It's like a craze.
Miss Yates	But a dangerous one. I'd best be off. [*She indicates a line of pupils outside his door.*] Looks like you've got some customers.

SCENE THREE

Mr Ferguson's class of first years have now started their work. Mr Ferguson is going over a problem with Karl.

Mr Ferguson Look, if you divide this by three what will you end up with?

Karl I don't know . . . I can't do it.

Mr Ferguson Yes you can because it's the same as the one you've just done. Work it out in the same way.

[Karl *picks up his pen which* Mr Ferguson *instantly recognises as one of the missing pens.*]

Is that your pen Karl?

Karl Yeah . . . er . . . yes sir.

Mr Ferguson Where did you get it from? Come on lad don't waste my time. Where did you get it?

Karl I got it off one of the third years. She said her dad gets them for her.

Mr Ferguson So she gave it to you. Very generous don't you think?

Karl No, she didn't give it me . . . I paid her 10p for it.

Mr Ferguson Out of your dinner money no doubt. Come on – the Head will want to see you about this. You're going to have your first singing lesson, little bird!

Karl Sir?

SCENE FOUR

The four culprits: Rani, Karen, Aaron *and* Sam *are now in the* Head's *office. On her desk are the stolen pens.*

Head I suppose you know why I have called the four of you out of your lessons? I don't have to tell you that there has been an alarming number of thefts in the school recently, do I? Of course I don't – because you know more about them than I do, don't you? You know exactly when they happened because you were there at the time, weren't you? And you know how much was taken because it ended up in your pockets, didn't it? . . . Well?

Aaron It weren't us Miss . . . we never.

Head I presume you wouldn't mind saying that to the police then Aaron?

Karen You haven't called the police, have you?

Head No Karen, I haven't. Not yet. But if you are not prepared to tell me exactly what you have taken and also to return those things to their owners, then I shall undoubtedly have to call in the police.

Karen Please don't Miss. You don't know what . . . what.

Head	Karen, I don't think you need to tell me what I do or do not know! What I unfortunately do know is that four of my pupils are thieves. Yes, it's a nasty word isn't it? . . . Well, you'd better get used to it because that is what people are going to think of you now. You can, of course, convince them otherwise – but, I warn you, it takes a long time. You are going to have some time to think about what you have done because I am going to suspend the four of you from school for the next two days, after which time I shall see you and your parents.
Karen	Please Miss . . . don't tell my Dad . . . he'll . . .
Head	Karen! That is all; you may go now.
	[*As the four pupils leave the office Miss Yates enters.*]
Miss Yates	Trouble?
Head	Well, yes and no; at least we found who our light fingered brethren were.
Miss Yates	Oh dear. And was Karen Woods one of them?
Head	Yes. She seemed very upset by the whole thing. Especially when I said they would be suspended for two days – she was almost in tears.
Miss Yates	I'm not surprised; she certainly will be when her father finds out.
Head	Her father?
Miss Yates	Yes. I'm afraid he has a history of beating both Mrs Woods and Karen. When he finds out she's been suspended . . . Well I wouldn't like to guess what his reaction will be. Isn't there any possibility of lifting the suspension?
Head	That would be extremely difficult. We would be seen to be favouring one person.
Miss Yates	[*gloomily*] And of course, half the school knows what they were in your office for, don't they?
Head	Not only that; I had a call from one of the parents just before you arrived. She wanted to know what the school was doing about the recent spate of thefts. I told her that we had discovered the culprits and they would be dealt with severely.
Miss Yates	So everyone knows who they are and what they've done. They're just waiting for us to punish them.
Head	Yes. And you're asking me not to punish one of them.

FOLLOW-UP

1 Discussion:

a) Which of the people in the play do you blame for the situation?

b) Do you think Karen should receive the same punishment as her friends?

c) How do you think they will react if Karen is not punished?

d) Why would the Head find it difficult to decide what to do in this case?

e) What would you do?

2 Improvise and/or write the script for the final scenes of the play.

Quickies

I think

Sit together in a circle. Each person thinks of a school rule that they agree with. Going round the circle each person says. 'I think the rule about . . . is a sensible one because . . .' The second time round everyone thinks of a rule that they don't agree with. This time it's, 'I think the rule about. . . is stupid/ annoying/unnecessary because . . .'.

School dinners

Sit together in a circle. Choose three different types of food which are served up in your own school at lunchtime. (If the food is such that it has gathered nicknames you could use them.) The leader gives out the food names at random around the circle until each person has one of the three names.

When the leader calls out, for example, 'chips', all those who have been given the name 'chips' must run round the outside of the circle until the leader gives the signal to return to their places. The last one back must drop out. The game is won by the last person to be out.

What's the rule?

Sit together in a circle. One person goes out while the others decide on a rule. When the outsider returns he must try to find out the rule by asking the others questions about themselves. The rule can be a simple one – for example, answering the question as if you were the person sitting on your left or right, or pulling your left earlobe before answering the question.

That's a new one!

Work with a partner – A and B. A plays the role of the teacher, while B has to give the best excuses he can think of for not having done his homework – the more imaginative the better! Swop over when B runs out of excuses.

Starting Points

Sentence starters

Work together in groups. Take one of the sentences below and use it in a timed improvisation. One of the members of the group must use the sentence somewhere in the improvisation:

What are you doing?

You're always making trouble for us.

What do you mean, you were only doing what you were told to?

I'm not being rude but I just can't see the point of it.

No!

But I always eat my pudding first.

Sorry. If you haven't checked your tackle you don't have a go.

Making the rules

Work in groups of about eight to ten. You are a primitive tribe living about 100,000 years ago. Improvise a scene of a day in their life using the information given below. You will probably find that you have to make a number of rules to ensure the safety of the group, especially the children.

You live in hide tents beside a river. Your food is fish, meat and berries. Although the summers are long and warm it can get very cold in winter and at night. Although you have had fire in the tribe for generations, unfortunately the knowledge of how to make fire has recently been lost. There are plenty of fish in the river which is fast and deep. You hunt deer which can be killed easily with your bone spears. Many spears are used up during the hunt – this is a nuisance because they are tedious things to make. During the long summer there are plenty of berries to be gathered. Some are used for eating, some for medicine and some are extremely poisonous.

At the end of the session get together with the other groups and compare the kind of rules you found it necessary to make:

- did any of the groups make rules which were not directly related to the safety of the group?

- did any of the group members feel that the rules only applied to some people in the group? Was this fair?

- did any people in the group make rules that others would not like? How were they able to do this?

Prefect power (role play)

Work in groups of five.

CHARACTERS

Prefect
Pupil A
Pupil B
Pupil C
Teacher
(All the characters can be either girls or boys.)

SITUATION

One of the school rules is that all pupils other than fifth and sixth years must go outside during morning break. The sixth form prefects are responsible for clearing the building and making sure everyone obeys the rules. Although it is mid November and freezing cold outside, the rule still applies. Your teacher will give you further information.

How would you do it?

Work together in groups. Imagine that you live some time in the future. A new school has been built where you live and your group has been given the job of deciding what the school will be like. You have to decide:
- who will be able to go to the school.
- what will be taught in the school.
- what rules will be needed in the school.

When you are making your decisions you must keep in mind the following:
- every pupil must be able to find some success in his school life
- every pupil must be safe in school.

AUTOBIOGRAPHICAL

Correspondence

When a biographer sets out to write the story of someone's life they very often use letters which were written or received by that person. The letters you will find on pp. 44–9 are all about a young girl and her family. When you have read the letters improvise the scene that you think would follow.

Work together in groups. When you have finished, compare your scene with that of another group. How have they developed their characters? Are they different to yours?

FOLLOW-UP
Imagine what these characters would be like after ten years has passed. Write a letter for each character which reveals what has happened and how they feel about it. Put together a short production in which each character reads his or her own letter.

Quickies

Famous people

Each member of the class has the name of a famous person pinned to their back. The only way they can find out who they are is to ask questions of other people such as: Am I a man or a woman? Do I appear on television? Am I in politics? etc.

My life

Work together in pairs. You have two minutes to give your partner your autobiography. Make sure you include as many of the important aspects of your life as you can.

Now swop partners and tell your new partner your 'old' partner's autobiography. Find the 'owner' of the autobiography you have just heard and tell them what you know about them.

Approve/disapprove

Sit together in a circle. In the first round each person in turn tells of something about themselves that they disapprove of. You might say, for example, 'I disapprove of my tendency to talk too much.' What you say must be true. You can say nothing if you wish.

22 Southwick Road
Brunton

Mr S. Elphik
A.C.M. Records
44 Sandown Road
London NW3

15 July 1986

Dear Mr Elphik

A friend of yours, Oscar Nespen, advised me to write to you. He said you were looking for girl singers, especially those who were also instrumentalists.

Mr Elphik - look no further! I have been singing in discos with my own group for nearly two years now. I write my own songs and can accompany myself on either piano or rhythm guitar. I am very keen to make a career in the music business.

I would be very grateful if you could give me a chance to make a recording.

Yours sincerely

Suzi Brown

22 Southwick Road
Brunton
15 September 1986

Hi! It's me again. Thanks for the stuff you lent me for the disco we did. I think we must be getting better - at least that lot didn't chuck their plastic cups at us!

I wrote to that record producer Oscar told us about, but it was about a month ago now and I still haven't heard anything from him. I would have given him a ring but I couldn't find his number in the book - you don't think Oscar was kidding me do you? I mean, he talks about going on tour and making recordings in the South of France but he always seems to be around here or at his Mum's.

Got to go - they still insist I keep up with the music lessons..... it's so booooooooring!

Tara!

Sue

22 Southwick Road
Brunton

15 September 1986

Dear Ella

I'm sorry I haven't written for so long but you know what this house is like sometimes — madhouse is a better word.

I had a letter off Susie's Headteacher yesterday saying how worried they were about her. Apparently they had their careers forms to fill in and she'd put on hers that she wanted to be a rock singer. It's not even as if she's dim - the Head said all her subject teachers say she'll do really well in her exams - could go to university if she wanted. He's coming to see us tomorrow night about it.

And on top of that my aunt Enid is coming over for a few days. I don't mind - poor old thing, she doesn't have much of a life, but she gets on Ken's nerves. I don't suppose she means it but every time she opens her mouth she's criticising him over something. The last time she came he went off down to the pub in the end saying, " I always knew World War Two must have been my bloody fault." As you can imagine I'm not looking forward to any of it.

Bye for now. My love to the family
Mina

The Laurels
West Heath
Rinsdorp

14 September 1986

My Dear Mina

I am so looking forward to seeing you and the
family on Saturday. My train will arrive at Brunton
Station at 3.30. I will get a taxi from the station
in order to save Kenneth the trouble of starting
his car — or perhaps he has a new model by now?

I shall bring with me the de-caffeinated coffee
and other things which my doctor has insisted
are necessary for my condition so there will be
no need to try to find them in Brunton, which
does seem a little short of specialist shops.

I hope Susan is well — I am so glad you
encouraged her to keep up her music. So
few girls these days seem to care for it.

Best wishes to you all.

Aunt Enid

**LYNWOOD GARAGE
WARLEY AVENUE
BRUNTON**

15 September 1986
Mr K. Brown
22 Southwick Rd
Brunton

Dear Mr Brown

I regret that you did not answer my previous letter concerning the payment for your new car which you purchased from us on 12 August 1986. Since that time a further payment has fallen due and has not been paid.

At the time of writing you owe this company £179. If this amount is not paid within the next 14 days I will have no alternative but to repossess the vehicle and begin court proceedings against you.

I trust you will resolve the matter satisfactorily.

Yours sincerely

R. T. Seller (Sales Manager)

Evelyn Page School of Music
Andover Crescent
Brunton

12 September 1986
Dear Mr Prescott

Thank you for your letter about Susie Brown. I can quite see why you would be concerned about Susie's career choice – I agree with you that a modern pop singer certainly does not have a secure future. I also agree that it is often only luck that brings success to musicians.

However, Susie is a very talented and determined girl – if she wants to be a rock singer then I have very little doubt that in one form or another she will be just that.

If I know anything about Susie she will make up her own mind and nothing will change her.

Yours sincerely

B. M. Ketzler
Director

The second round is for approval. Each person tells of something about themselves of which they are proud. You could say, for example, 'I approve of the way I offer to help at home.' Again what you say must be true, and again, you can say nothing if you wish.

Crystal ball

Work in small groups. Imagine ten years have passed. Describe yourself as you think you will be then. The others can ask you questions about your life during the last ten years.

Starting Points

Uniqueness shields

You will need large sheets of paper and felt tip or marker pens for this.

Like the Round Table of the knights of King Arthur, your shield cannot be used by any other person. In order to make the shield completely yours, invent your own coat of arms to decorate it with.
You could:
- design a symbol to represent your name.
- write a motto or an epitaph for yourself.
- include your greatest success and/or failure of the year.
- put in your hopes for next year, or ten, or twenty years from now.

FOLLOW-UP

Make a uniqueness shield for your family, or your whole class, or a team or a club you belong to.

I'd like you to meet

Work in groups of about ten. You have all been invited to a party. One person will take on the role of the host or hostess. As each person arrives at the party they will be introduced to the others.

You have to act in whatever character the host/hostess gives you. For example, they may say, 'I'd like you to meet . . . her new book on dinosaurs has just come out.' In this case you would obviously have to take on the role of an author of a book on dinosaurs and answer all the questions that the other guests will put to you.

Take it in turns to act the role of host/hostess.

FOLLOW-UP

Begin to address other people in the role you want them to adopt. For example, you could go up to someone and say, 'I've always wanted to meet an executioner/long distance hopper/maggot collector. Your work must be very interesting.' The person you speak to must take on whatever character you describe.